I Know Myself as Thief

Jo-Ann Iannotti, OP

I Know Myself as Thief

Jo-Ann Iannotti, OP, Author and Photographer

Email: hello@orenaugmountainpublishing.com
Website: www.orenaugmountainpublishing.com

First Printing 2025

ISBN: 979-8-9925369-1-1

Cover photo by Jo-Ann Iannotti, OP

Printed in the United States of America

For my parents, Mae and Anthony Iannotti.
None could be better.

My heart wants most of all to steal their silence.

From “Reading Other Poets”

The Call

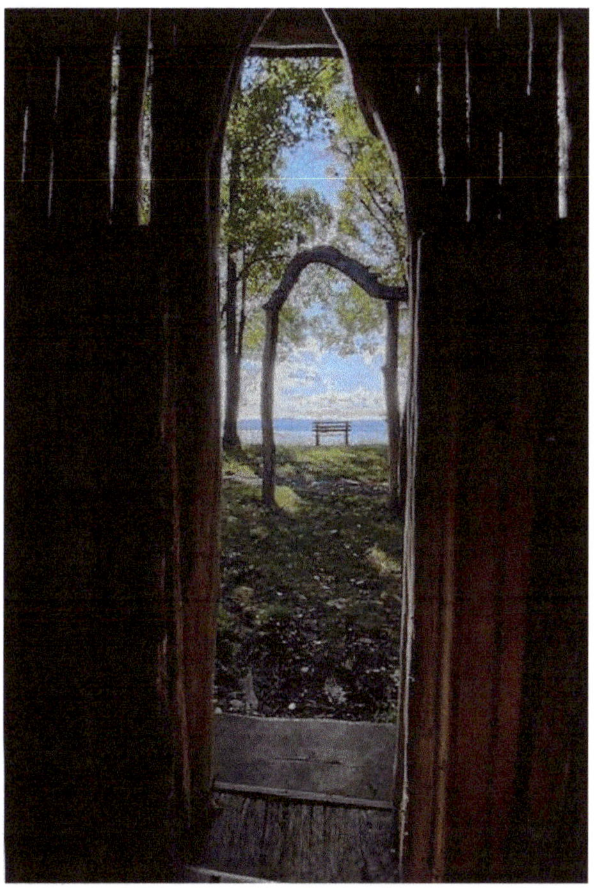

I cannot tell anymore when a door opens or closes,
I can only hear the frame saying, *Walk through.*

—Ada Limón
From “Sharks in the Rivers”

Just a Moment of Silence

Just give me a moment of silence,
a time to call my own,
a time to sift all worries,
a time to wake what's known.
Just give me a moment of silence,
and, I'll show you one who's grown.

Paterson, New Jersey, 1962
First poem

Table of Contents

Foreword

When Sr. Jo-Ann asked me to write the foreword to her book of poems and photographs, I was honored. I don't remember when we first met but, at that time, I didn't know she was a nun—a Dominican Sister of Hope. I had seen her and Sr. Rosemarie at concerts and community meetings, and there was something about her that drew me to her. Perhaps it was experiencing her effervescent joy or listening to her speak with clarity of thought.

Later, when we began having conversations about politics or poetry, Thomas Merton or Pema Chodron, I felt I was making a friend for years to come. We collaborated in the development of arts programs at Wisdom House, such as "Readings in the Gallery." And, when I was director of the Litchfield County Writers and Artists Project at the University of Connecticut, I invited her to present a show of "Word and Image"—poems and photographs—and to talk about her creative process.

Through these bumpy years of democracy, we continue to discuss the way forward as artists, realizing in this time of crisis that some are set on silencing our voices. The clarity of Jo-Ann's poetry, like her photographs' clarity, makes visible through her listening heart what is invisible to the eye.

She admonishes us in her poems to "Wake up." She cautions us, "Don't make fear your refuge." This advice goes beyond the boundaries of any specific religion or philosophy. In her photographs we can see into the life of things. In all her work, revelations lead to transformations through clarity of sight and speech.

Davyne Verstandig
Professor Emerita,
University of
Connecticut
April, 2025

Preface

The arts bring us to truth about ourselves, others, and life itself.

They take us by the hand and lead us to where we need to go. They befriend us, and are faithful even when we wish they wouldn't be.

Reading poetry and writing poetry, taking photos and quietly taking in others' photography, made me want to see like they saw. I became a poet and a photographer. It was then I discovered that I had been both all along.

These two arts have formed me to approach life in a different way.

I'm ever grateful to my father for being willing to buy me *The Sunday New York Times* in the 1960s. To spend an extra $1.00 on this teenager, when for another 50 cents he got both *The Daily Mirror* and *The Daily News*–which had the funnies included–for the rest of the family!

I would read the Book Review section of the *Times* and want to write like those writers did. Words came from a close listening as I read contemporary poets like Robert Frost. The Dominican Sisters I had in school encouraged the writings that I would do for school publications.

Each Sunday, I would spread the ads for Lord & Taylor women's suits and dresses on the kitchen table and try to recreate the sometimes full-page sketches. I wanted the skill out of which their art was born.

Photos would come years later as I used the photography of others as my own personal tutors. What came from catching an angle, seeing something ordinary in a new way, made me want to get closer because there was more to see. And, because light moves so quickly, immediacy was the key. What started as attraction led to closer attention.

So, this present collection of poetry and photography is the result of years of listening from a place of silence. They were born from silent observation and obedience to silence. And, these many years later, I continue to want to steal even more of it.

I am an active practicing thief knowing that the booty is bottomless!

Jo-Ann Iannotti, OP
April, 2025

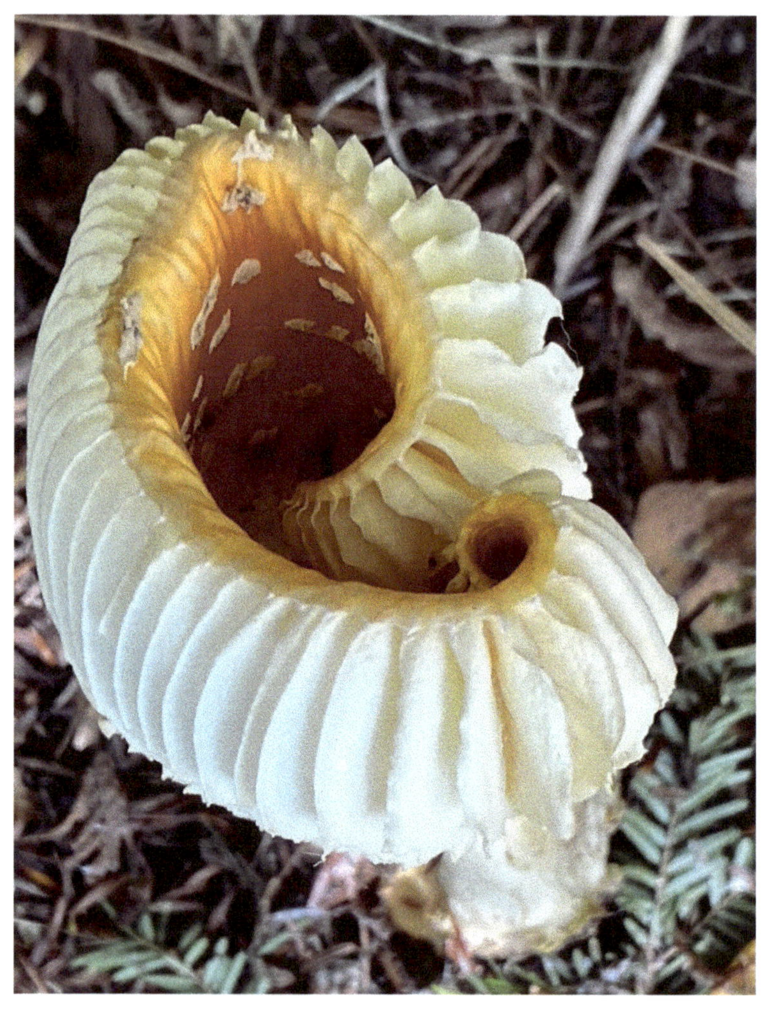

A Position of the Heart

He seduced the Cross
	into making love.
He coaxed it,
	pressed it to himself
	until
it was difficult to see
	which had initiated
		the embrace,
	which was making
		the offering.
And
	which one had
		actually
			given in.

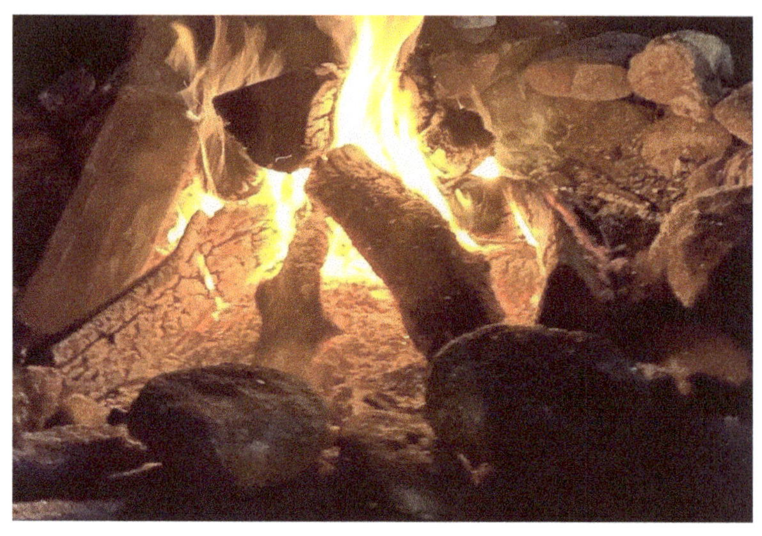

The Thirst

Flame
  becomes
fire
  when
dried wood
  is prepared
to have a thirst
  satisfied.

All Shall Be Well

ALL SHALL BE WELL
Words: Jo-Ann Iannotti, OP (adapted from the Revelations of Divine Love
by Julian of Norwich)
Music: Rosemarie Greco, DW

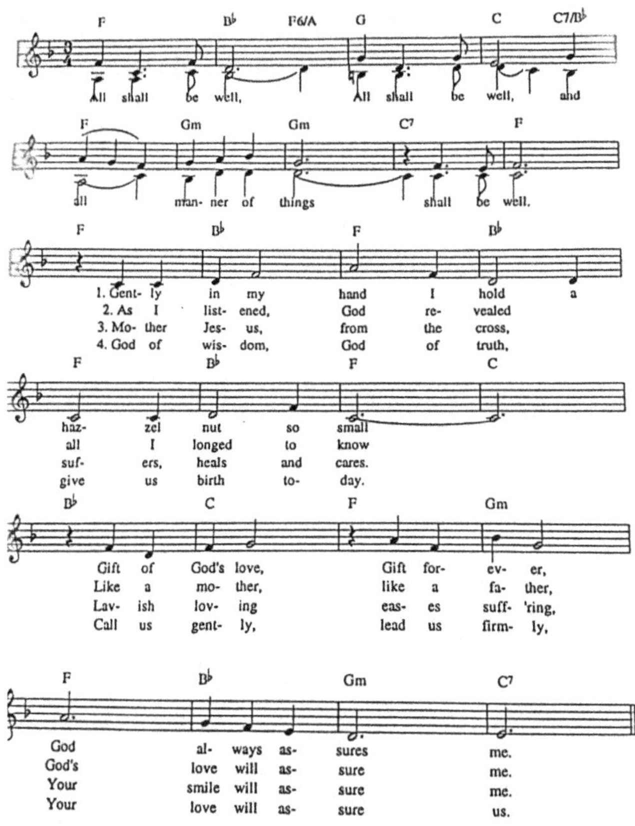

All Shall Be Well

All shall be well, all shall be well, and all manner of things shall be well.

1. Gently in my hand, I hold a hazelnut so small,
   gift of God's love, gift forever,
   God always assures me.

2. As I listened, God revealed
   all I longed to know,
   like a mother, like a father,
   God's love will assure me.

3. Mother Jesus, from the cross,
   suffers, heals, and cares,
   lavish loving eases suff'ring,
   your smile will assure me.

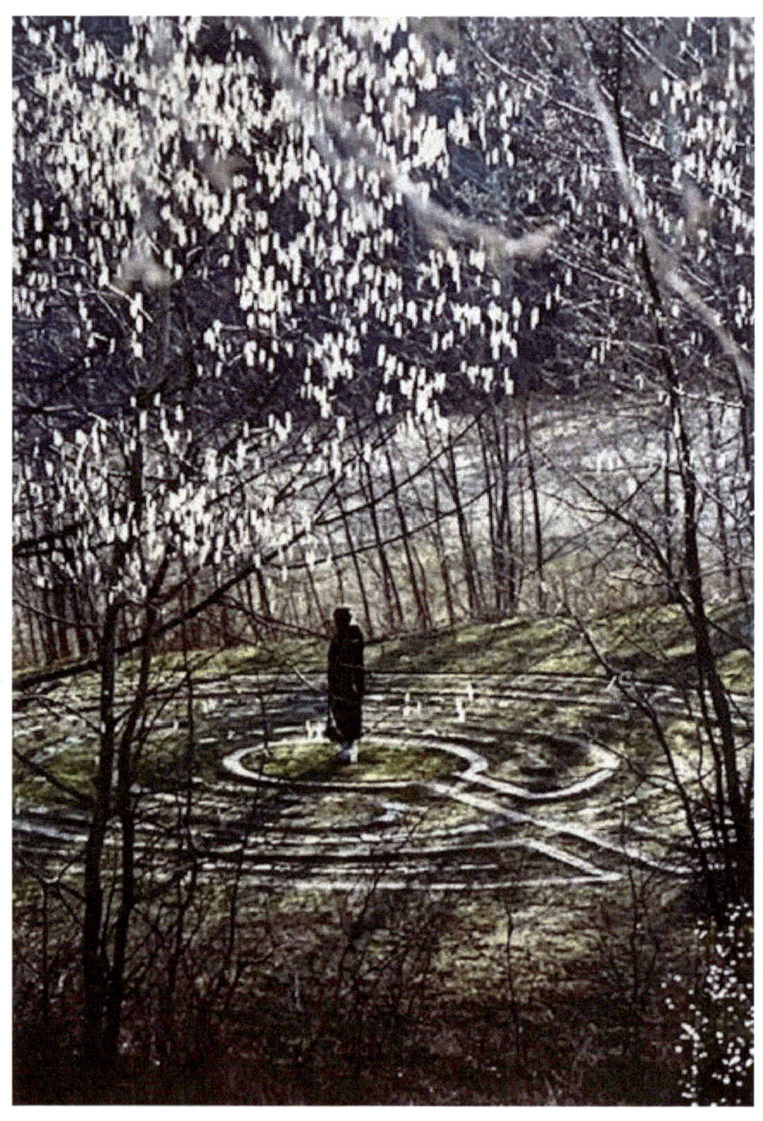

4. God of wisdom, God of truth,
   give us birth today.
   Call us gently, lead us firmly,
   your love will assure us.

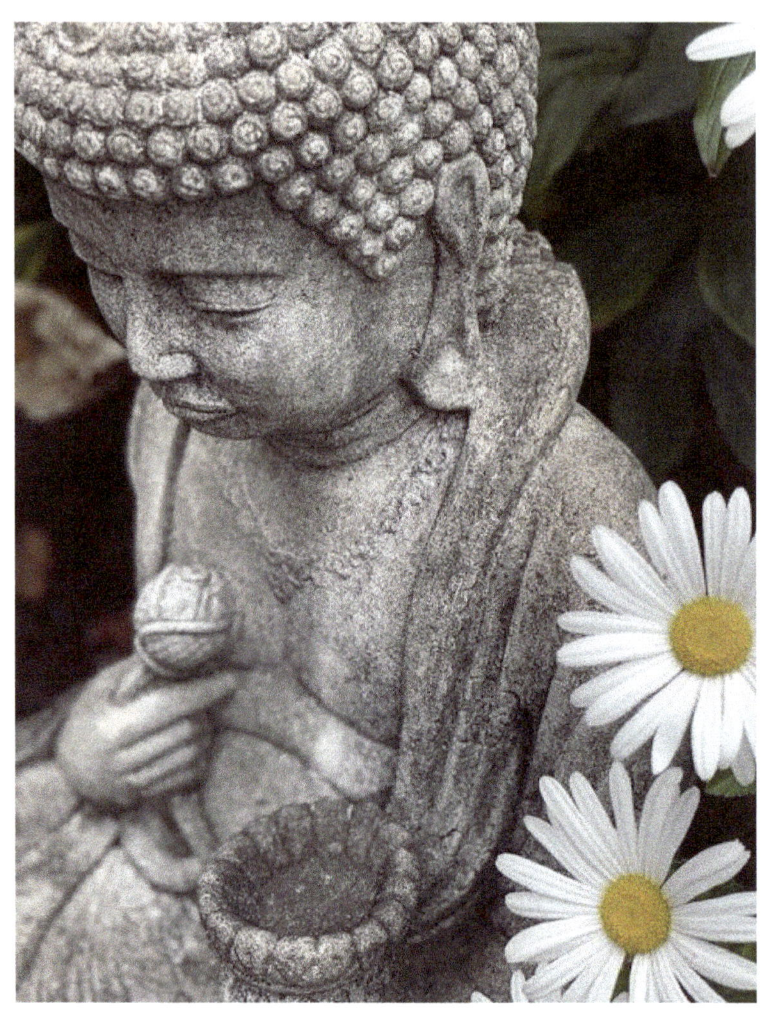

Reading Other Poets

When I sit in awe at the sound of
their words,
listen to the journeys of
their hearts,
walk in the richness of
their memories,
I know myself as thief.
I know the envy in
my heart
wants, most of all,
to steal
their silence.

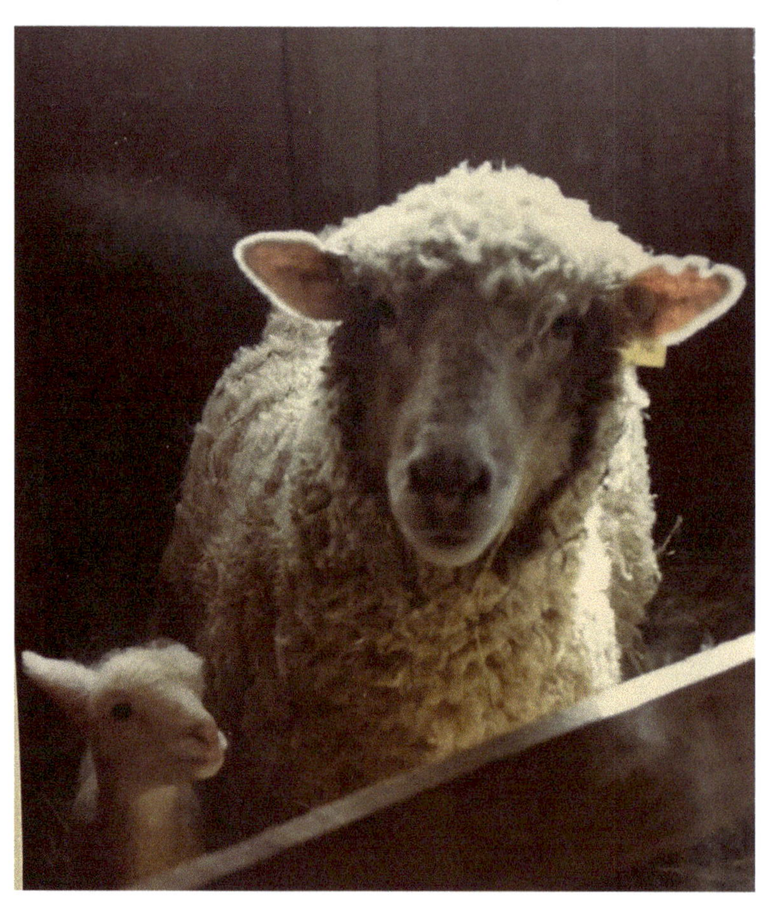

Motherhood

Pregnant robin
  protecting
new life
  hops
with one eye
  looking
    behind.
Inside the barn
     the ewe understands.

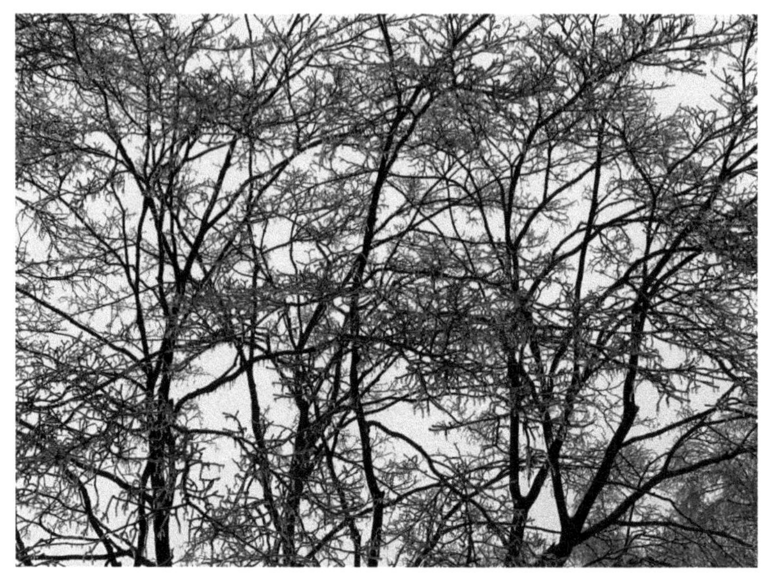

Love

Love strips
to the
bone
to unveil
the
heart.

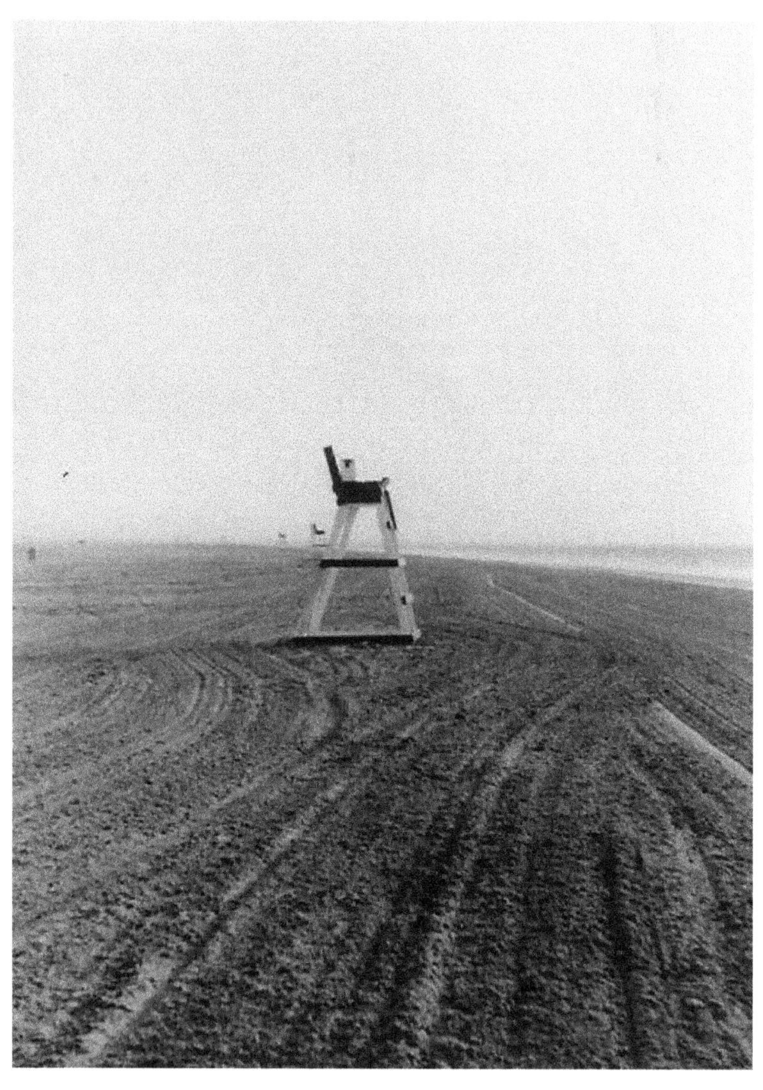

My Annual Olympiad

(Getting past my mother's anniversary)

I want to get through it
    champion-like.
Stoic simplicity. Smooth passage
    over each stroke of memory,
  having in my cells
    a rote response,
Clear, uncluttered,
  that nothing can disturb
   hair, eyelash, or tear duct.
Dare I mention her name?
 Dare I bend over to someone and say,
  "Today's her day"?
 Can I take it?
Can I sift through dreams
    and find her now?

*(poem unfinished)

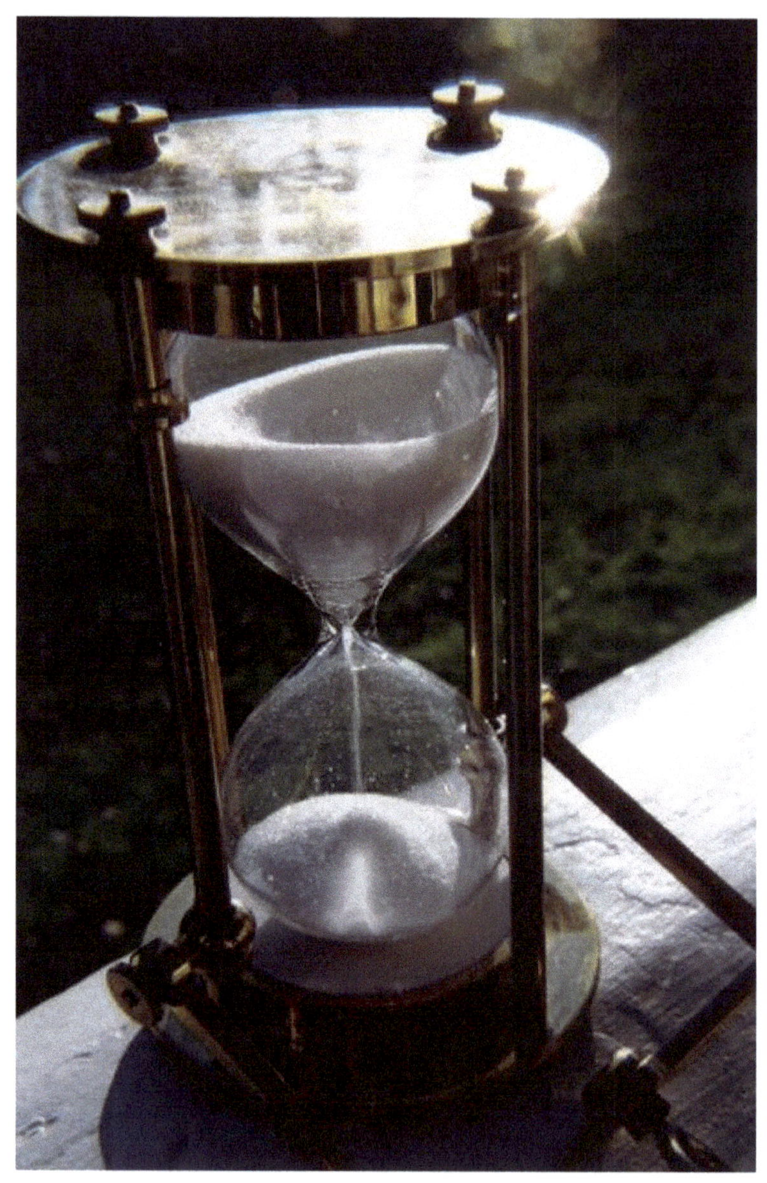

Remembering 9/11

In the city Walt Whitman called,
"City of hurried and sparkling waters!
City of spires and masts!
City nestled in bays! My city!"
The twins were born and razed.
No one expected them to die together.

Then, the bastion defined and designed by
geometry,
A place whose angles held secrets
supposedly secure,
had its impenetrability shattered.

Finally, in a field, in one of the original 13,
still called "Keystone,"
a field made to be ploughed
had the unfulfilled hopes
of 40 souls planted in its sod.

Seemingly secure was that day in September.
sun-filled, mild-mannered in its dawning.

Before mid-morning, day became nightmare.
Chaos reigned supreme, and the dust of
humanity
was a veil over the City.
Faces covered with the mask of ash.

That day, more than names were listed as lost.
That day, futures were frozen in time.
Nothing could move forward.
That day, Belief was a sign hung around our
necks
With the simple message—"For Sale."

Bent steel bent lives into new shapes.
They were placed into a furnace
of transformation.

They were too surprised to make a rational
decision.
Never given the chance to choose.

Now, 20 years on and more, the meaning is still a
challenge
to our once-innocent souls.
What remains is the power of re-membering—
coming together again
and again, making room for new loves to
flare up in us.
All of life is kindling for revelation.
So, friends, stack it high.
Build it well.
And, let us start a new fire
for gratitude, for clarity, for truth,
for life!

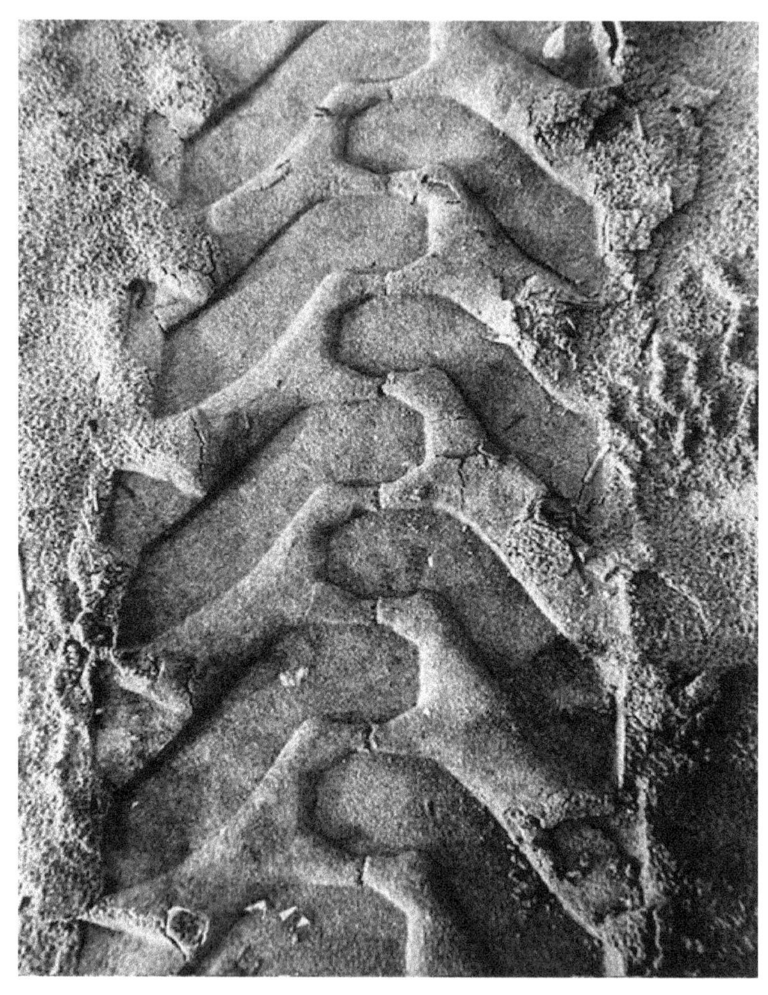

Summer Rains

Warm
moist the
waiting.
Slowly
the earth's body
postures
to be loved again.

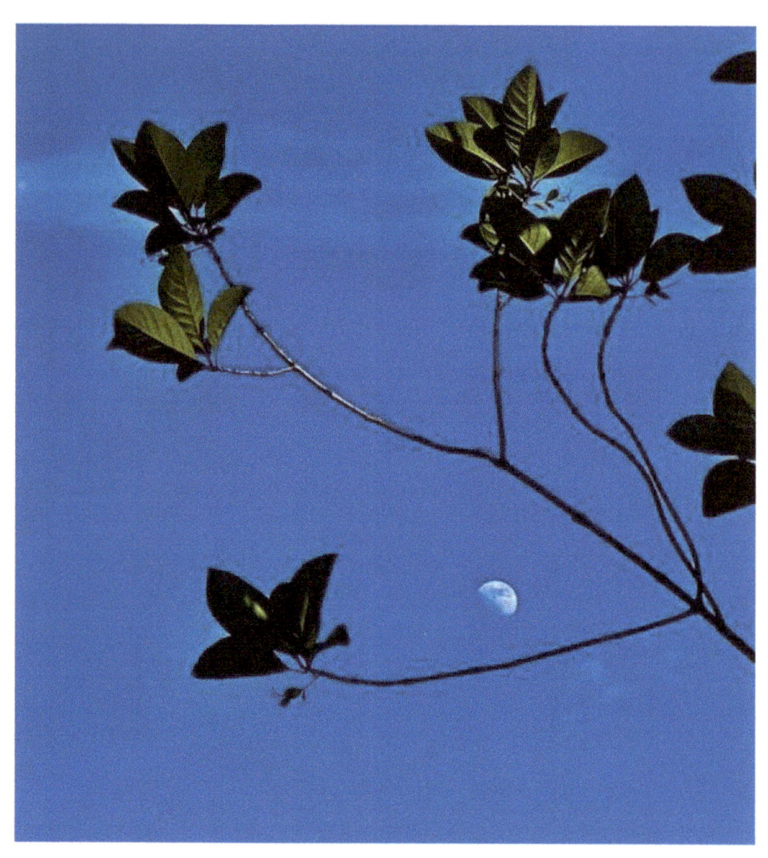

To Have Reached Out

To have reached out
        for a point
so high that the
sky looks
        up
to it,
  is to have
        yearned for
what is in
        our reach—
                          mysteriously.

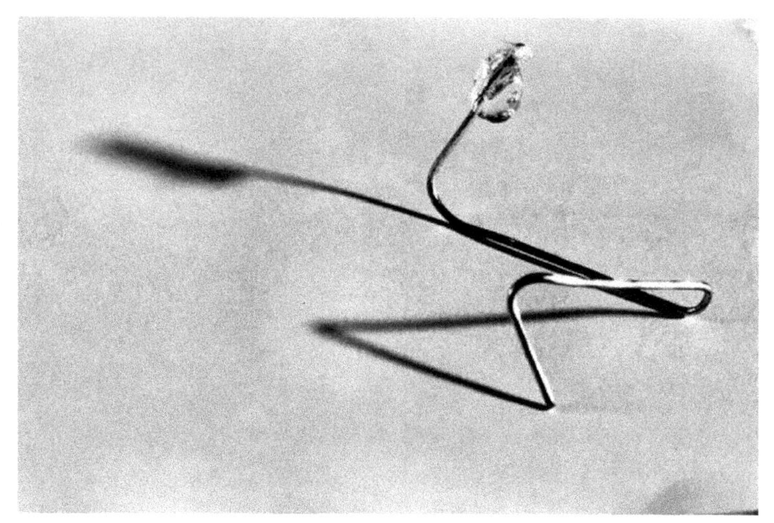

Eucharist

Breaking bread
at angles
of entrance
never to be
closed again.

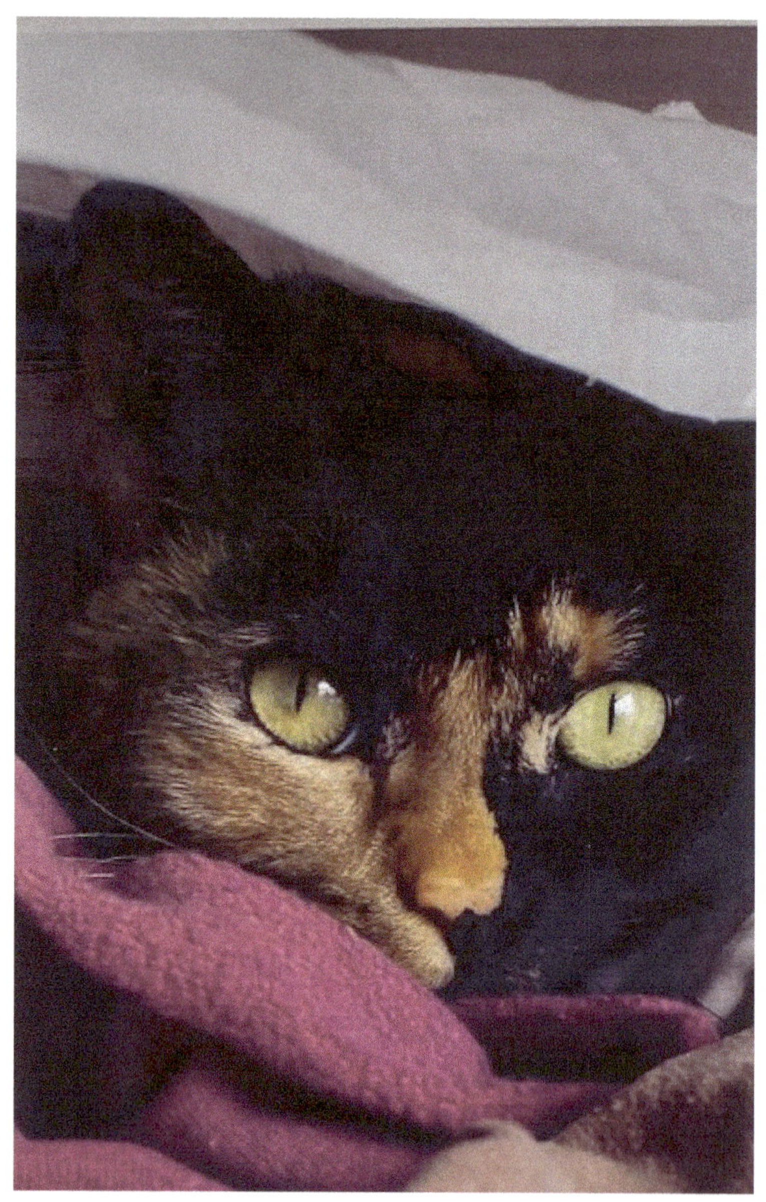

Eavesdrop My Heart

(For R.S. Thomas)

Lean as close as
you can
to catch the
pronunciations
of each beat.
They will be slow
at first
(knowing you are there),
Hesitant until
they
trust
you will not
want to
change their rhythm
or
demand a new
vocabulary

to suit greener ears

and

hearts not yet unhusked

by the searing

of love.

Winter

Winter stormed in tonight
    with the audacity
of a prodigal:
smothering all established
    life forms
under the freezing blanket
of a snowfall.

Days have passed with
    no indication
of its arrival.
Nights have gone by
    wrapped in the
moderate winds of late
    autumn.

We have been conquered.

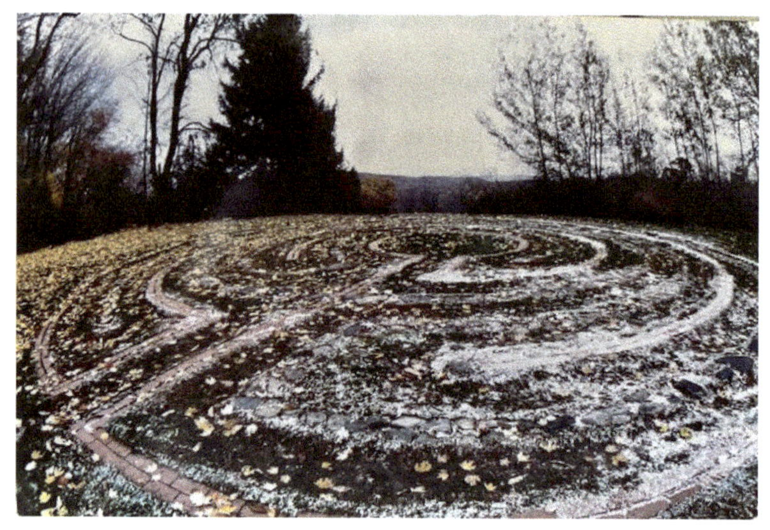

No longer do we
belong to in-between
seasons.
An all-certain
Winter
has us in her grips.

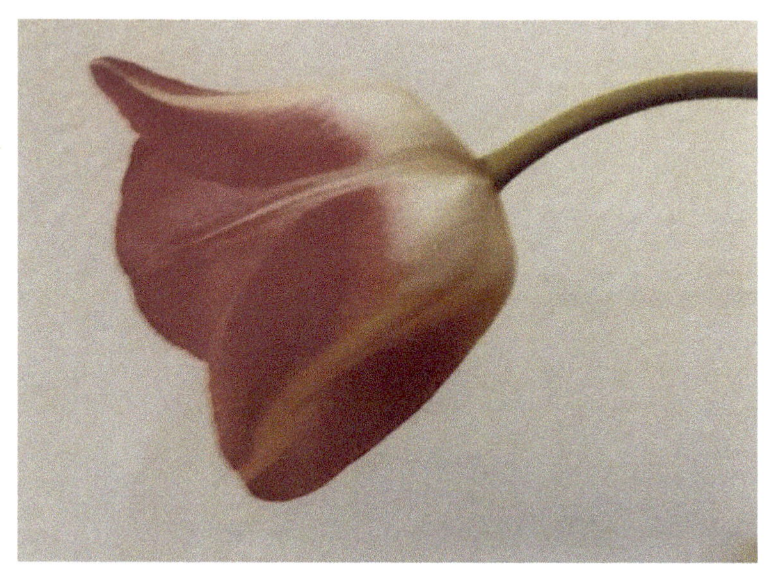

No One Has to Teach

No one

has

to teach

Nature

how

to bow

Before the mystery

of

this night.

Christmas, 2019

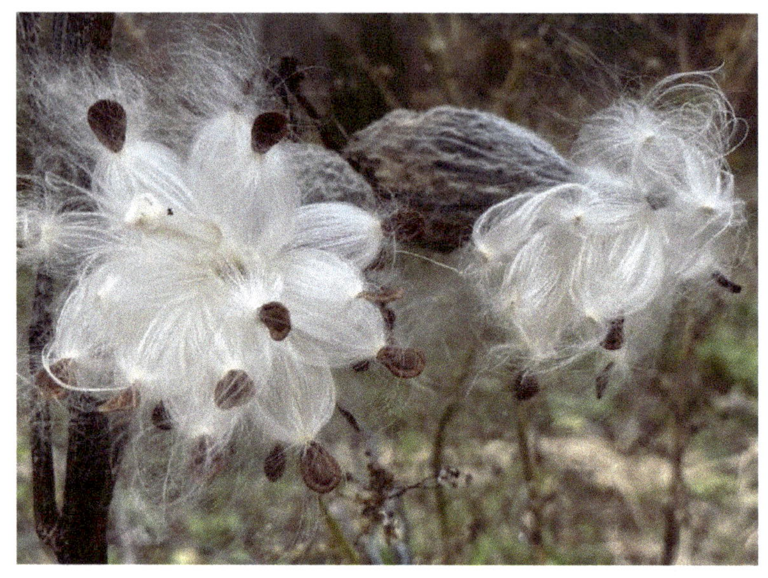

Annunciation

Love whispers
in monosyllables.
"Here," "Now," "You,"
And the heart nods
"Yes."

Luke 1:38

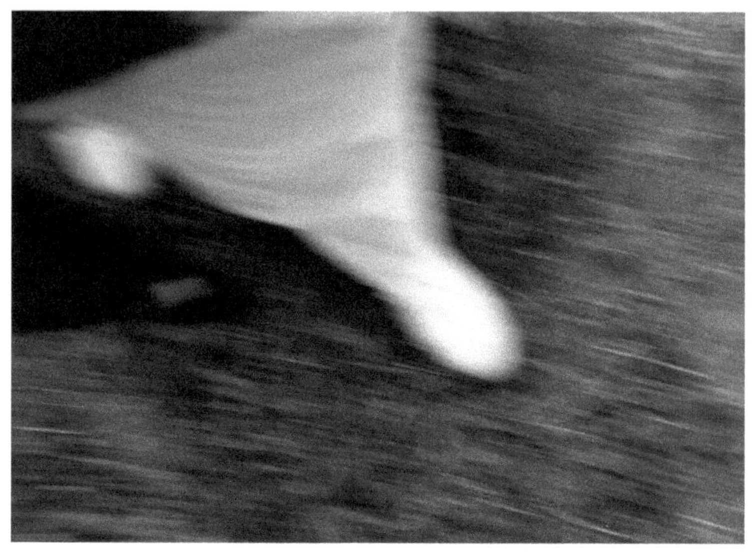

In Via

There is joy that
comes with
early spring rains as
they drench furrows
still wearing the frowned
brows of
winter discipline.

The human presence now
takes the form of
footprints pressed into
soft earth telling
tales of one who is
on pilgrimage.

The nights and days of pilgrims
intersect with
the promise of a star-filled

progeny
and the uncertainty of what
may appear on
an unguarded horizon.

Wake up, look for signs that
help is on the way,
probably even arrived.
Coax out salvation
hiding among the rubble.
Give it
new clothes to wear,
a ring for its finger,
and the fatted calf for the
week-long celebration.

Don't make fear your refuge.
Don't be paralyzed
Into believing a fixed center

is a true home.
Seek the home that
doesn't leave you
When you have to move on.

The journey and the pilgrim are one.
Traveling and expanding
deepen
Planting into greater understanding, into
a more fertile union.

Who showed you the road
to take,
the gear to pack?
The longer the journey,
The less baggage
you need.

Be true to the path

despite
unexpected detours.
Don't mistake detours
for wrong decisions.
The way is laid out
in pieces
not always closely
connected.

At each point along the way,
greet strangers
who do not have another's love
To enfold them.
Freely give the oil
of forgiveness,
Wine of compassion,
and bread of promise.
You will find many waiting
for a new mercy,

to listen to their hearts
crying in the night
over lovers lost to battles
there was no
chance of winning.

Their dreams bring them
home
to familiar lands
buried beneath
generations of living simply
on the top. They have been
waiting their turn
to show their faces and
claim their inheritance.

Now is the time to reclaim
what was lost.
The chosen ones sacrifice

themselves
for their younger brothers.
Sisters
walk hand in hand
as the strength
of their mothers links them
flesh and marrow to the seeds
of future life.

So, don't turn around for the
consolation of yesterday.
Mud has already been scraped
off souls encrusted
by temptations of indifference.
The orchard
has been pruned in readiness.
Aching limbs
look forward to the harvest.

The vision has been readjusted
    to tomorrow's light.
Look, it comes slowly
    on the horizon,
wearing the face of the
    blood-red grape,
carrying the dove
    in its white wounds,
planting slips of new life.

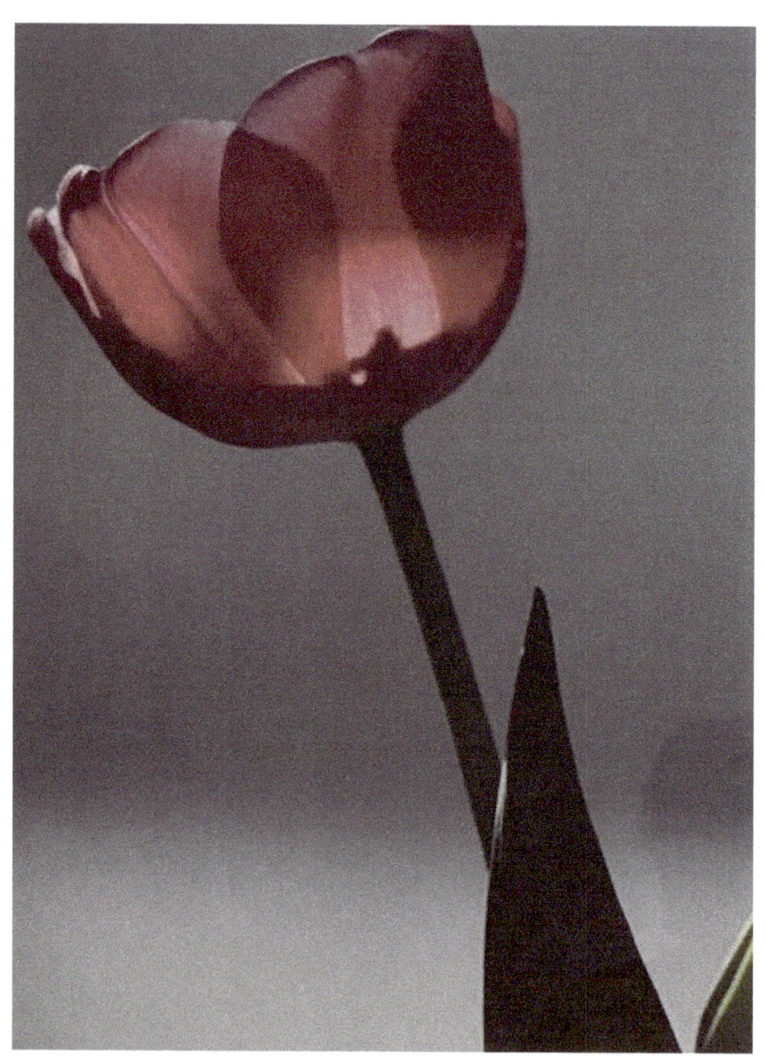

The Virtue of Sin

I have learned

more about

grace

through sin

than in

the practice

of

virtue.

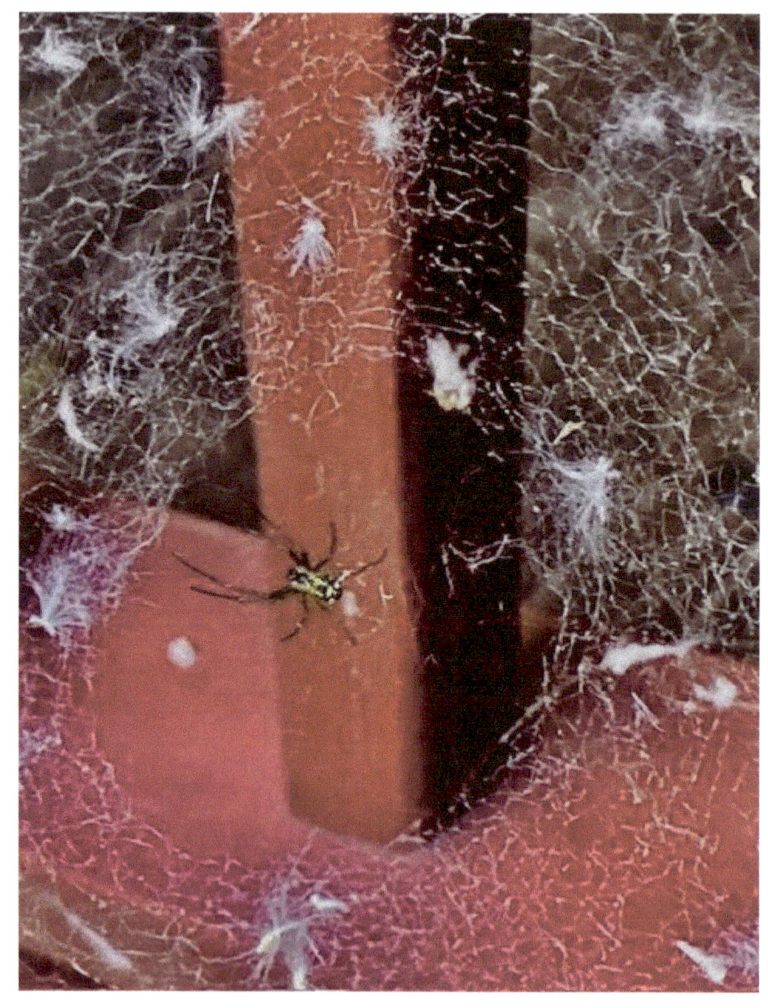

Them

The people I love the best
  are those who throw
   caution to the wind
when the wind is not
     at their back,
          but
biting their nose
         and closing their eyes.
Sometimes their real name
       scares even them,
But, they wear it tattooed
       on their arm
and, then go out and buy

a whole new wardrobe

of only sleeveless

shirts.

Unthinkable

The angelic body bowed low
in adoration
before the woman soon-to-be-
with child.

"Blessed," he called her.
"Why?" she asked.

"Chosen" was his answer.
He waited. She wondered.

"How? Not now," she said.
"God changes time," said
the messenger.
"A son but no husband?
A mother before
being a wife?"

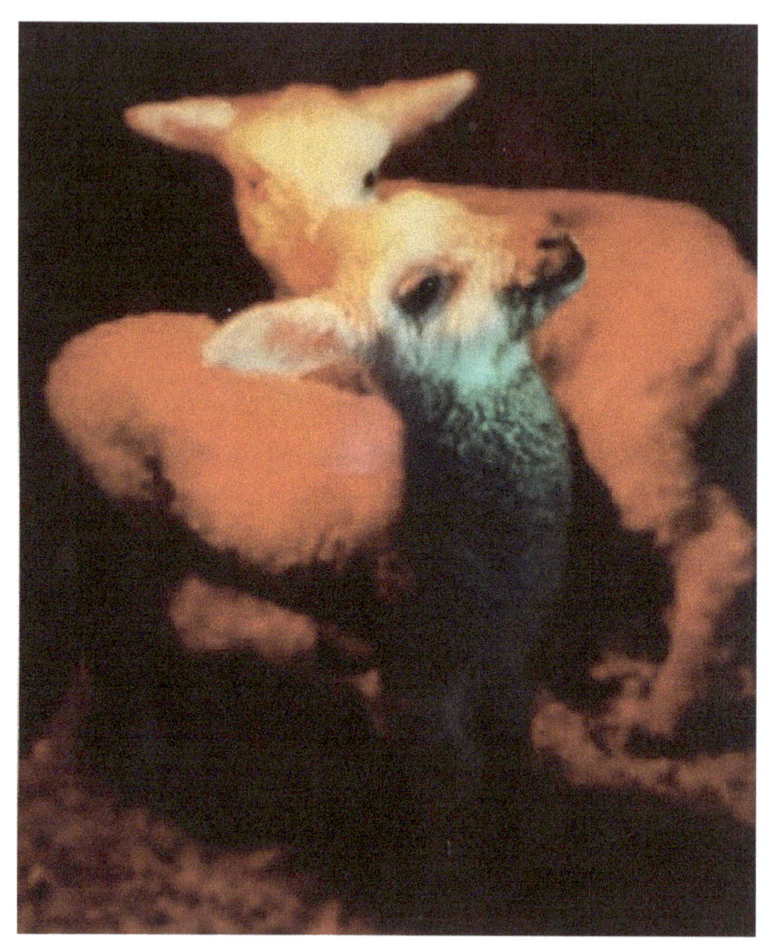

"Impossible" she pro-

tested.

"Exactly," he smiled.

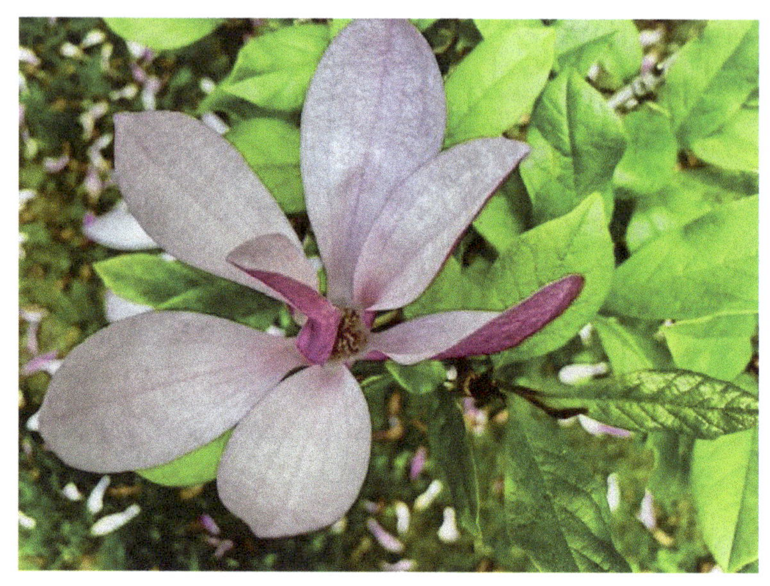

Ahhh!

I have been looking for a reason to thaw,
        to unfold into the truth.
Petals of perfection
        stretch into the light
intoxicating the eyes,
        and, relax in resurrection.

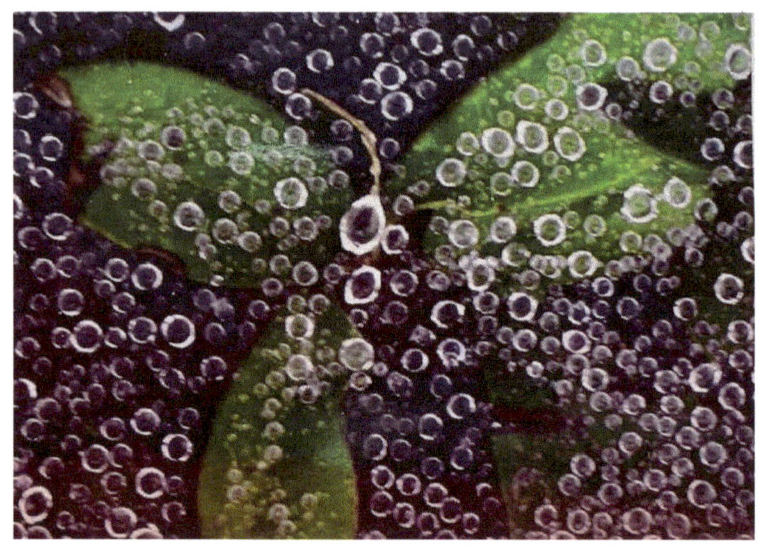

Gently,

you came as unseen rain.
not unfelt,
not without the taste
of
refreshment.
just unseen.

No intensity of looking
ever guarantees
finding you.
Only yearning,
sometimes tears,
never letting go.

Silent Meditation

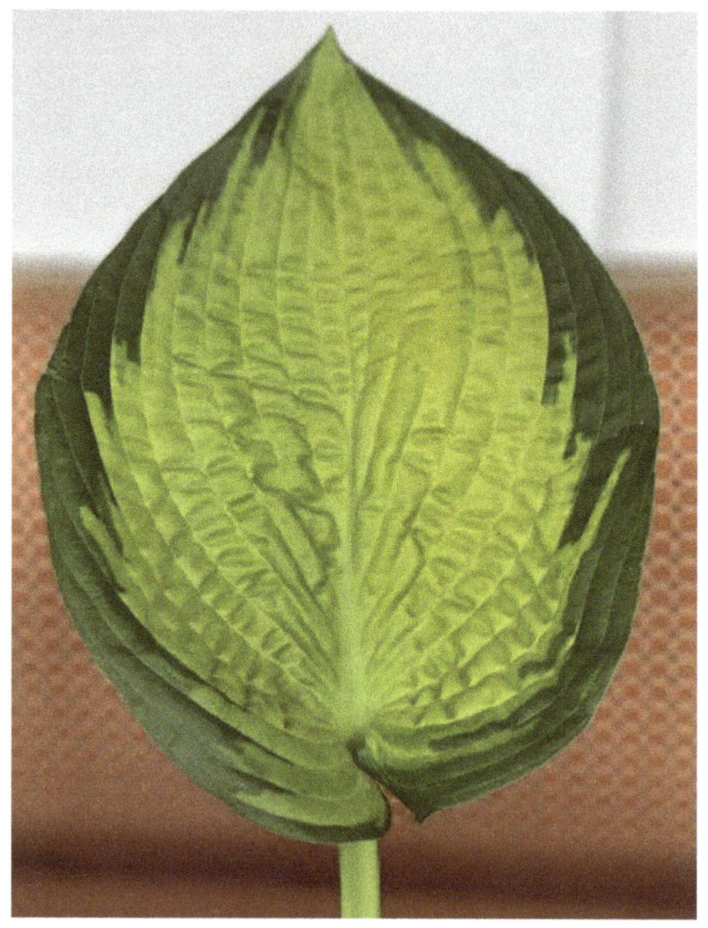

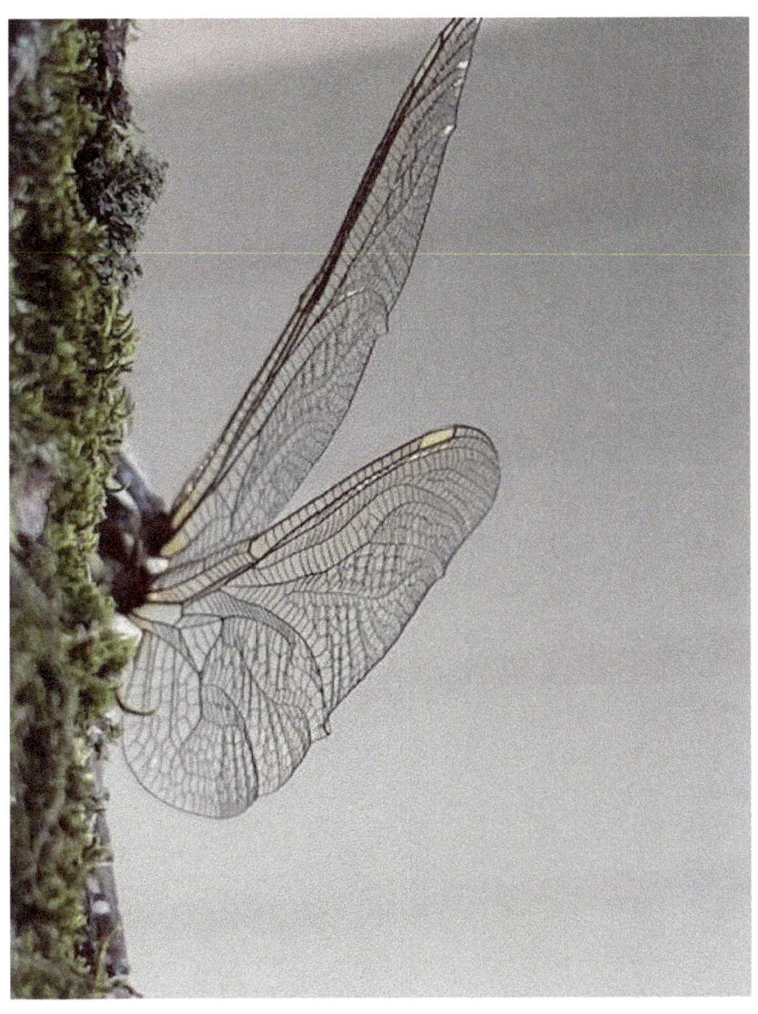

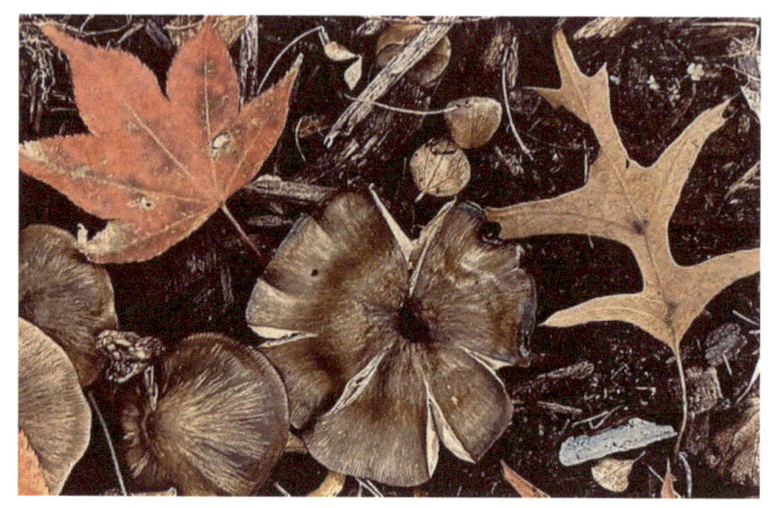

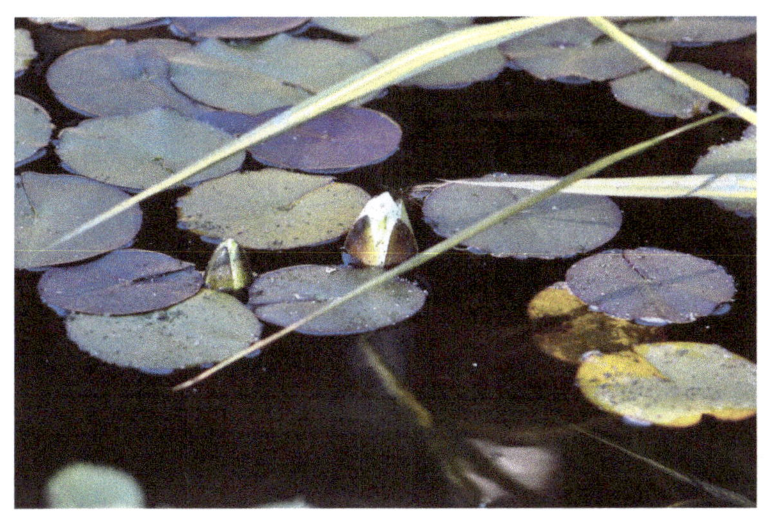

Permissions

Peter Lobo, OP, editor of *Dominican Ashram*, to reprint the following poems:

> "A Position of the Heart," *Dominican Ashram*, March 1985, Vol. 4, No. 1, p. 9.
>
> "Gently," *Dominican Ashram*, March 1990, Vol. 9, No. 1, p. 24.
>
> "The Thirst," *Dominican Ashram*, September 1990, Vol. 9, No. 3, p. 140.
>
> "In Via," *Dominican Ashram*, March 1994, Vol. 13, No. 1.
>
> "Reading Other Poets," *Dominican Ashram*, June 1994, Vol. 13, No. 2, p. 53.

Review for Religious

> "To have reached...", July 1977, Vol. 36, No.4, p. 599, Saint Louis University Libraries Digitization Center.

Photograph of Jo-Ann Iannotti by Ruedi Hofmann provided courtesy of Wisdom House.

Acknowledgments

Heartfelt thanks to:

Marie and Ken Ford for their enthusiastic and generous support of this project,

Sandy Carlson, who patiently guided the process of the creation of this book with vision, precision, and an artist's eye,

Oliver Wolcott Library in Litchfield for the space and quiet needed at various stages in the process,

Deborah Kelly, executive director of Wisdom House Retreat and Conference Center, for providing a location that continuously supports the arts,

Adrienne Bendzinski, marketing coordinator at Wisdom House, for sharing her technological skills,

Davyne Verstandig, Jack Gilpin, Rabbi Rami Shapiro, Julia Cameron, and Judith Petrovich, artists in their own fields, whose commitment to their arts has inspired me for many years,

My community, the Dominican Sisters of Hope, for encouraging my efforts to share our charism of preaching through the arts, and

Rosemarie Greco, DW, musician and my collaborator in many artistic ventures, for suggesting we create a song to honor the Revelations of English mystic, Julian of Norwich.

About Jo-Ann

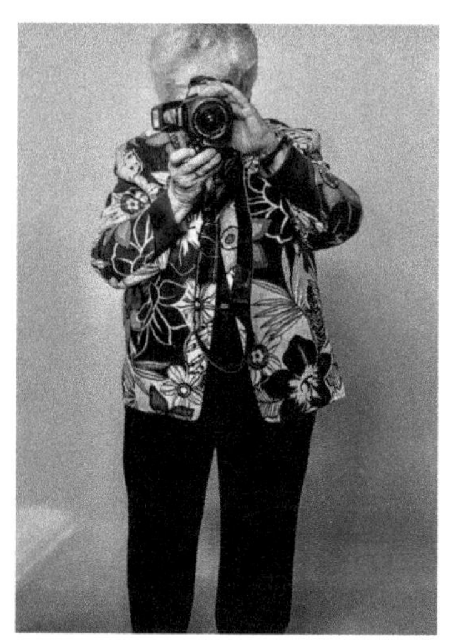

Jo-Ann Iannotti, OP, is a Dominican Sister of Hope living in Litchfield, Connecticut. Jo-Ann is a poet and photographer, and her poetry has appeared in national and international magazines. A member of the Dominican Institute for the Arts, she has had solo shows of her photography in New York and Connecticut.

Jo-Ann lectures frequently on the 14th-century English mystic Julian of Norwich as well as the interrelationship between art and spirituality. She is the author of *Remember, Return, Rejoice: Journeying from Ash Wednesday to Easter Sunday*. She frequently serves as a supply preacher for numerous churches in northwestern Connecticut.

Her ministries have included being art and spirituality coordinator at Wisdom House Retreat and Conference Center in Litchfield, associate director of vocations for the Archdiocese of Hartford, a script writer for the Office of Radio and Television of the Archdiocese of Hartford, and reporter and photographer for *The Catholic Transcript* newspaper in that archdiocese. She also has taught in elementary and secondary schools in New York and New Jersey.

A native of Paterson, New Jersey, she holds a BA in education from Mount Saint Mary College, Newburgh, New York, and an MA in theology from Fordham University, Bronx, New York.

Reviews

"Jo-Ann Iannotti, OP, wears a triple vocation. She is a devoted religious, a gifted photographer, and an even more-gifted poet. In her collection *I Know Myself* As *Thief*, she celebrates all three callings. Deeply felt, her poems have a stunning simplicity. Her photographs capture precisely the natural world. Her voice, at once humble and authoritative, speaks through all. An artist to her fingertips, she reveals the sacred to be found in all creation."

—Julia Cameron, author of *The Artist's Way*, playwright, novelist, and filmmaker

"Imagined dialogues with angelic messengers, the virtue of sin, and eternal mysteries make appearances in Jo-Ann Iannotti's evocatively titled *I Know Myself as Thief*. The poems are inspired by day-to-day occurrences, recollections of world events such as 9/11, and individual responses to loss and love. Through her poetry and photography, she offers us a multi-layered experience of memory and emotion, stirring recognition and familiarity."

—Judith Petrovich, photographer

"These poems and photographs by Jo-Ann Iannotti are deeply inspirational. They are the work of a true artist, giving us piercing glimpses of the creative, loving presence of the Divine in this world we live in every day. I will always treasure this book."

–Jack Gilpin, actor and Episcopal priest

"Jo-Ann Iannotti's photos pull you from the surface seen to the depths felt. Her poems unfold the deep, revealing a fleeting world lit by words and permeated by spirit too close to touch. Don't read this book. Savor it."

–Rabbi Rami Shapiro, author of *Accidental Grace: Poetry, Prayers, and Psalms*

www.ingramcontent.com/pod-product-compliance
Lightning Source LLC
LaVergne TN
LVHW052348100826
845147LV00012B/782

* 9 7 9 8 9 9 2 5 3 6 9 1 1 *